FREE TO PRAY

UNDERSTANDING PRAYER

SHAQUIDA ANO

ISBN: 978-1-7329900-5-0

Printed by: A&C Marketplace Publishing LLP in the
United States of America

Cover designed by: Angela Miles

First Printing, 2019

TABLE OF CONTENTS

INTRODUCTION

Have you ever questioned whether or not God really hears your prayers? Do you find yourself wondering if you are praying correctly? When in prayer, do you struggle to find words to say? Have you ever heard others pray and secretly desired their prayer ability? Perhaps, it appeared they had all the right words to say, or their prayers seemed eloquent and powerful. They prayed longer or louder and to you, the prayers flowed just perfectly. Do you reach out to others to pray for you because you have confidence in their prayers which causes you to minimize your own prayer ability? If so, you are not alone! Many believers do not have confidence in their ability to pray and see their prayers answered. We identify a select few people who we believe are able to pray and touch the heart of God on our behalf and we designate them as our prayer warriors. What if I told you that you too have the ability to pray and get a prayer through to Heaven? You too have the ability to pray and see a manifestation of your prayers answered! You too are a vessel of prayer! Free to Pray was written to eliminate the mindset that causes one to believe that only a few are called by God to pray. This book will thrust the reader into a posture of bold, faith-activated, effective prayer.

Let me tell you about Grandma Emma. Grandma Emma was a praying woman. She was the anchor and pillar of our family. She taught us everything we needed to know about God. Grandma

Emma prayed every single day. We even knew her prayer times. She had two consistent prayer times. The first thing she did in the morning was drop to her knees and pray. If we entered her room while she was in prayer, she would look up just for a moment to sharply dismiss us. Her second time of prayer was right before she went to bed. She had us all trained. We knew not to disturb her during her prayer time. Prayer was her lifeline. At the time, I couldn't understand anyone needing to pray so much. I thought she was being a little extra. My sister and I laughed about her peculiarity when it came to prayer. Her bedroom was her sanctuary. I will never forget how immaculately clean it was. We were not allowed to play in her room and we could only sit on her bed when approved. She was very particular. Thinking back on it now, I realize that her bedroom was the place where she met with God. It was the place she prepared to spend time with Him. She made her room comfortable for a King's presence. Her bedroom was the space she dedicated for her and God.

We were a very close knit family. We often came together to eat and fellowship. Before eating meals, Grandma Emma would pray over the family and bless the food. We never knew what to expect from her prayers. Sometimes, it was a simple blessing and more times than not, we couldn't tell if she was praying or preaching. She would end the prayer compelling us to repent and instruct the adults to teach the children about God and to raise them in the church. She loved us so much and you could hear and feel it in her prayers. The one thing that was certain to us was that she knew how to pray and what to pray, for her family. We trusted her prayers. When we needed prayer and guidance, we called on Grandma Emma. If Grandma Emma said it was going to be okay, I knew it was going to be okay. I knew she heard God. We saw her consistency in prayer and her love for God and His people. Over the years, we witnessed her prayers being answered. Her loved ones got saved and generational cycles were broken. She even prayed my mom and I out of abusive relationships. She never stopped praying for us. Even on her death bed, she was praying for us. She transitioned to heaven with a smile on her face like she had seen God. She was our Angel, our prayer warrior. I believe her prayers were answered, not because she was special or better than anyone else. I believe they were answered just because she said yes to God's will in prayer. She didn't pray what she wanted, she prayed what God wanted. There is a difference. We will discuss this later in the book.

James 5:16 states; "Confess your sins one to another so that you may be healed. The earnest prayer of a righteous person has great power and produces wonderful results." The phrase to look at is; "righteous person." This scripture implies that the righteous person can pray and see a manifestation of answered prayers. The question is; "Who is the righteous person?" Those who believe in Jesus the Son of God are the righteous. Those who desire and strive to live our lives in a way that pleases God, are the righteous. Those who love God are the righteous! We all have the ability to pray and see God's will manifest by way of our effectual, fervent prayers. If you have struggled in your prayer life or get weary in waiting for an answered prayer, it is possible you have the wrong mindset concerning prayer. By reading this book, you will gain a clearer understanding of God's heart concerning prayer. You will learn that prayer is not meant to be difficult, but can be accomplished with simplicity. The reader will develop a basic understanding of why we pray. You will gain insight on fasting and prayer and how to fast effectively. You will learn the benefits of praying the word of God opposed to praying from your emotions. By reading this book, you will gain confidence in Holy Spirit and learn to submit to His guidance in prayer. You will learn what it means to be an intercessor and get an understanding of the heart of an intercessor and so much more. If you have struggled with prayer in the past and you want to grow in prayer, this book is for you. YOU ARE FREE TO PRAY!

CHAPTER 1

IN THE BEGINNING

Grandma Emma introduced me to God in 1993 at a young age, but I drifted away. I was 12 years old when I confessed Jesus Christ as my Lord and Savior. Unfortunately, I rebelled and drifted away from God for several years. It wasn't until 2008 when I felt the pull of God on my heart to return back to him. I'll never forget my financial, spiritual and emotional condition at the time. I felt exhausted. I was drained from the struggles of life. Everything that could go wrong was going wrong and I couldn't see a change in my future. I couldn't see the light at the end of the tunnel. I remember visiting the church of my childhood pastor. All I wanted was hope. On that day, it felt like the message was personalized just for me. I'm not sure how many people felt the power of the word that day, but judging from the number of people at the altar, half the church did. At the end of the message, the altar was flooded with people. As the message was coming forth, I couldn't hold back the tears. It felt like every word spoken touched my heart. I was overwhelmed in a good way and just needed to release what I was feeling with a good cry.

After taking that walk down the aisle, I rededicated my life to God. I decided that there would be no more delay. It was my divine time. I felt God speaking to my heart, saying; "Now is the time daughter." I gave him a Yes! I wanted to please God. I wanted to yield my life to Him. Not only did I rededicate my life to God, I joined the church shortly after. I wanted to learn about Christianity and how to live a life that was pleasing. I didn't want to be a Christian who confessed God with their mouth, but did not live a life that He was pleased with. I knew it would take some time. I knew I needed to be taught and I was willing to sit under a pastor and learn. I started attending service on a regular basis. I went to Sunday school and Bible Study weekly. I was really happy with everything I was learning. I was changing every day. It wasn't always easy, but I was sold on the idea of serving God wholeheartedly. The more I got to know God through the reading of His word, the more I wanted to know about Him. In my zeal to learn more, I began to follow in my Grandma Emma's footsteps. I read the Bible every morning and every night before going to bed. I remember some mornings I would run late for work because I was so engrossed with the word. I was like a kid in a candy shop. I was amazed by what I was learning about God. At night, I would go downstairs and read for hours. My husband would come downstairs and insist I come to bed. I heard many messages preached from the pulpit, but there was nothing like reading the word for myself. Nothing could compare to my private time with God. God's word spoke to my heart!

One of the areas I wanted to really grow in was prayer. I wanted to learn how to pray. I would pray in the morning and night, but I often wondered if God really heard my prayer. I listened to the prayers of the preachers at my church and I was impressed. They seemed to always have the right words to say. Their prayers came out so eloquently. They would pray loud and hard and it just seemed so powerful to me. I knew for sure that they were the prayer warriors. There was one woman whose name was Donna. Donna was a powerful woman of God. Every time she opened her mouth to pray, it seemed like mountains moved and heaven opened up. I was drawn to her. I knew she had a real relationship with God. Donna was a true servant. She worked tirelessly in the church. She could sing, dance, preach and pray and she was beautiful inside and out. The anointing of God was all over her. She was also over the Tuesday night prayer meetings. Every Tuesday, the church held corporate prayer services. I wanted to attend, although I felt I didn't know how to pray. I felt that I was drawn to prayer and oftentimes I would pray for others in my quiet time. I wanted to attend the prayer service but I was fearful. I knew that if I went to prayer service there was a possibility I would have to pray out loud. I knew that they pulled people out to pray. I was not having that! I was comfortable with praying at home but I was not ready or willing to pray in front of others. The thought of it made me nervous. My small prayers were nothing in comparison with the roaring lion prayer warriors at the church. Every time I thought of attending, thoughts of standing in front of people holding the microphone praying and not knowing what to say, plagued me. I was not ready to be embarrassed. For months, I fought against the desire. Fear and pride held me captive.

After approximately five or six months of fighting the desire, I finally worked up the boldness to go to prayer service. The entire ride to church I was praying, begging God not to be put on the spot. My heart was beating fast. I was extremely nervous. From the time I pulled up to the church and walked through the doors, I prayed. In my mind, I was saying; *"Please, please, please, God don't let them bother me!"* I just wanted to sit in my seat and pray silently, but I also wanted to learn how to pray by listening to others. I knew that if you wanted to learn to do something, it was best to surround yourself with people who knew how to do it. However, to avoid being called upon, I decided to sit in a corner with my head down the entire time. Even if they wanted to call on me, I wanted them to believe that I was already in prayer, hoping that they would leave me alone. On this particular night, when I walked in the door there were only two people there. Donna and her husband. I walked in and went straight to a seat in the corner and I waited for prayer to start. I was praying that more people would show up, but they didn't. With only the three of us there, I knew it was a strong possibility that they would call on me. I thought, if they called on me, I was going to leave. I was just that fearful! After a few minutes of sitting, Donna got up and grabbed the microphone. She opened up with praises. She began to thank God and sing songs of gladness to Him. She began to roar! It felt like she prayed for everything and forever. I thought; "Wow, how did she learn to pray like this?" I was impressed! I was a babe at the time, so everything seemed amazing to me. As Donna prayed, she paced the floor back and forth as I sat in the corner with my head down, praying in unison with her in my heart. Each time I felt her walking pass me, I got nervous. I dreaded her touching me on the shoulder and giving me the microphone to pray. Eventually she walked next to me and didn't move. She stood right beside me and continued to pray. I was shaking. I knew it was coming. My head was down. I refused to make eye contact. I didn't have to because she kindly tapped me on my shoulder. I looked up and she handed me the microphone and said; "You Pray!" I was horrified. But in that moment, I had a choice to make. Would I go forth or would I decline? In that moment, I decided to put my fear and pride to the side and obey the woman of God. I thought I would just talk to God the same way I did at home. I took the microphone and walked to the front of the church and I began to pray.

There are a number of questions to be asked here. Why was I so fearful to pray? I believe one of the primary reasons was because I had the wrong understanding or no understanding of prayer like many of us. I was never taught the foundations of prayer. I was bound by fear, pride, comparison, insecurity, and more. The Bible declares in *John 8:32 "And ye shall know the truth, and the truth shall make you free."* The truth spoken of in this Scripture is the message of Jesus Christ, the Son of God. In Him we have freedom. We are no longer slaves to fear! *"We can do all things through Christ who strengthens us" (Philippians 4:13).* A believer should not be bound by anything! We must have a proper understanding of prayer or we will find ourselves frustrated and defeated in this area.

In the next Chapter we will discover:

What is Prayer?
Why do we pray?

CHAPTER 2

WHAT IS PRAYER?

Let's first take a look at "What is prayer?" The English word "pray" means to make a humble request to God. Prayer is a way to communicate with God. The best way to describe it is: prayer is a conversation with God. Prayer is communicating what's on your heart and mind and allowing God to share His heart and mind with you. So often we go into prayer with a checklist of things we want to say to Him. After a few minutes we are done and go to the next. We never sit and wait for a response from Him. It is unnatural to have a one-sided conversation. Those conversations are not beneficial. Prayer is a two-sided conversation between you and God. It is time specifically set aside just for a conversation with Him. It can be done anywhere! The Bible says; *"Here's what I want you to do. Find a quiet, secluded place so you won't be tempted to role play before God. Just be there as simply and honestly as you can manage. The focus will shift from you to God and you will begin to sense His grace."* Matthew 6:6 (Message Bible)

This scripture makes it clear that prayer should be done in a private, secluded location. We need time away from everything, just us and God. Prayer can be natural. It does not have to be dramatic. God is not so concerned about how you pray. The question remains, Do you pray? He prefers time spent with you and He will teach you all other things concerning prayer. He wants your undivided attention, which we give Him by going to a quiet place. He desires for us to release the stress and anxiety of the day and focus on Him. You can relax in prayer. You can take your time. Don't be in a hurry when praying.

Let me give you some simple steps to assist you with prayer.

- Identify a place for you and God (home, park, car).

- Identify a set time (morning, night, lunch break).

- Show up every day to that location at the appointed time.

- Take your Bible, pen and pad and worship music, if needed.

- Release all of your worries (ask Holy Spirit to help you clear your mind).

- Replace the worries by thinking on the goodness of God and all He has done for you and your family. Fill your mind with His goodness!

- As you begin to focus on Him, give Him thanks and praise will flow from your heart.

By following these simple steps, you will begin to enter into prayer. Write down what you hear God say to you or what you are sensing in prayer. Even if you are not sure it is God, write it down, journal your thoughts after prayer. It is good to write what you're hearing. For example, you could be praying for your finances and God may tell you to continue to give and trust Him so that He can add increase to you. If you obey Him and there is a manifestation of the increase, you can go back to your journal and look at the date God gave you the word. This will help you to build faith in God and better identify His voice.

Now that we've identified what prayer is, let's examine some of the top reasons why we pray.

The most important reason we pray is because prayer is the bridge by which we develop a relationship with God. In order to truly build a relationship with anyone, we must communicate with them. By communicating, we get to know them. The more we talk to them, the better we understand them and get to know them. It is like dating someone, the more you spend time together talking, the closer you get. It is the same with God. We must spend time talking to Him in prayer. We were made to connect to God.

The second most important reason we should pray is because the Bible instructs us to pray. As believers and followers of Jesus Christ we must obey God's word. If He gives us instructions, we must obey His commands. He is our Father and we submit to His authority. *1 Thessalonians 5:17 (Message Bible) says; "Be cheerful no matter what; pray all the time; thank God no matter what happens. This is the way God wants you who belong to Christ Jesus to live."* This means that prayer should be a daily discipline until we leave the earth. Once you build a relationship, you will understand the importance of obeying Him. Through relationship-building your heart yearns to please Him.

Lastly, praying is one of the vehicles God uses to enact His will on the earth. The Kingdom of God is voice activated. Everything on earth was created by the voice of God and the supernatural power of the Holy Spirit. We were made in God's image and likeness when we believed the Holy Spirit came to dwell in our hearts. In other words, He resides on the inside of us. We have the same ability to speak like God spoke in the beginning and according to His will, it will manifest. He has given us the power and authority to pray and speak things into existence. We will discuss more on this topic in a later Chapter.

CHAPTER 3

WHO SHOULD PRAY

As it was mentioned in the Introduction, many times we listen to the prayers of others and we are so impressed. Their prayers seem so powerful and these are the people we usually call on for prayer. It is great to call on people to pray for us. The Bible tells us to pray one for another, but we must not count ourselves out. As believers of Jesus Christ, we are all required to pray. We are all prayer warriors. The assignment of prayer has been given to every one of us, no exceptions. Every believer should have a consistent prayer life. We must reject the belief that says only a set group of people are called to pray. This thought causes elitism in the body of Christ. It causes people to feel that God hear others' prayers and not theirs or they can't reach God. The truth is, God hears all of our prayers. We all have the ability to touch God. The Spirit of God dwells on the inside of all of us. There is no one specific "elite" group that can touch God. We all can! While we all are called to pray, there are members of the body of Christ who have a greater burden for prayer. One of their major assignments on the earth is to pray. These people will usually be the ones who pray longer and more frequently. They may even pray with more insight and knowledge in certain areas. In prayer, they will usually pray with great passion and fervency. Passion is a strong and barely controllable emotion. Fervency is intensity of feeling or expression. People with a prayer burden will usually have an outward manifestation of strong emotions or expression. Prayer is their mantle. In the Bible, prophets were described as wearing mantles or cloaks. The mantle was a long garment covered in animal skin, usually sheep skin. The mantle was a symbolism of their office and authority. 1 Samuel 15:27; 1 Kings 19:13; 2 Kings 2:8. To make it plain, a mantle represents a man's gift, the call of God and the purpose for which God called them.

Many carry the mantle to pray which is typically accompanied by a supernatural grace or ability to pray. Let's examine this in the Word of God. *Luke 2:36-38 says; "Anna the prophetess was also there, a daughter of Phanuel from the tribe of Asher. She was by now a very old woman. She had been married seven years and a widow for eighty-four. She never left the Temple area, worshipping night and day with her fasting and praying. At the very time Simeon was praying, she showed up, broke into an anthem of praise to God, and talked about the child to all who were waiting expectantly for the freeing of Jerusalem."* In order to remain in the temple day and night praying, a supernatural grace from God had to be present. Many of us struggle with praying for one hour. It would be impossible for us to pray all day in our human strength. This can only be done with the help of Holy Spirit. Anna had a mantle to pray. She had a special assignment in the temple. Her assignment was to fast and pray and she eventually witnessed the manifestation of the promise of God. She witnessed the birth of our King Jesus Christ.

Everyone should pray, but not all will have as strong of a prayer burden as others. For example, everyone does not share the same burden for evangelism. An evangelist is a person who seeks to convert others to the Christian faith, especially by public preaching. All are called to evangelize, but an evangelist carries a greater burden and passion for souls and they typically bring in more souls than others. In the Kingdom, the primary purpose of the evangelist is to win souls. That is the area in which they will be more successful. To sum it all up, we as believers are all required to pray. However, one is not greater than the other. We are all equal, as God's children. He gives us gifts and callings by His Spirit. Those abilities are to help us fulfill our purpose in the earth realm. In fulfilling our purpose, His will is being manifested, which is the ultimate goal. Never get intimidated by the ability of how others pray. Be consistent in your private prayer life. Find out what your assignment is and become great at it. Remember, no matter what your gift, call or assignment is, you are required to pray and the God of our Salvation hears your prayers.

CHAPTER 4

"I DON'T PRAY LIKE THEM!"

A major hinderance to developing a prayer life is comparison. Oftentimes, I questioned if God heard my prayers because when I prayed, I didn't pray like everyone else. I was unable to pray in faith because I always doubted. I was afraid to pray out loud or around people because in my mind, in comparison, my prayers were weak. The statement I used was *"I don't pray like them."* God had to teach me. Holy Spirit revealed to me that I was looking at it all wrong. My mindset needed to change. In this Chapter, we will dig into the statement *"I don't/can't pray like them."* This concept is usually rooted in **fear, insecurity, feelings of inadequacy, pride, competition and comparison**. It does not stem from the pure love of God that compels us to pray. Let's look at the definition of these:

- **Fear** - An unpleasant, often strong emotion caused by the anticipation of awareness of danger. Fear will keep us stagnated and unable to move forward. Fear will speak to you and tell you, "If you pray, others will laugh at you." Fear is a form of bondage. Fear is sent by the enemy to kill your prayer life. *"God did not give us the spirit of fear, but of power, love and a sound mind."* 2 Timothy 1:7

- **Pride** - A high or inordinate opinion of ones' own self dignity, importance, merit or superiority. Pride will cause us to care more about our reputation and what people think of us, rather than obey God. We would rather be glorified in the eyes of people instead of humbling ourselves in obedience to God. Pride will cause us to resist prayer. Pride will cause us to depend on ourselves rather than depend on God to help us in prayer.

- **Comparison** - To examine two or more objects, ideas, people, etc., in order to note similarities or differences. Comparison will cause you to mimic others and lose your originality and authenticity in prayer.

Our God is an amazing God! When He created us He gave us all personality. Personality has to do with our individual differences among people in behavior patterns, cognition and emotions.

- God is creative. He made us all unique. No two people are the same. The fact that God uses us all differently is an expression of His awesomeness. If we all prayed the same, preached the same, praised the same, looked the same and thought the same, it would imply that our God is limited. God loves diversity (differences). Look at the rainbow. Visit the zoo and take a look at the animals around you. Take a look at the humans all around you. Even those who closely resemble have unique features. Prayer should be done according to your unique personality.

- Be You! Be Confident in your personality and in the way God uses you. Never give in to the temptation to mimic another persons' prayer style. The Bible tells us in *Proverbs 27:17* *"Iron sharpens iron, so a friend sharpens a friend."* I truly believe that we should learn from one another. I learned a lot about prayer by surrounding myself with people who were skilled in prayer. We will learn from others, but we should present it in our own unique prayer style. I assure you, God is not concerned about how loud or fast you pray. He's more concerned about the heart of the person that's praying.

- Keep in mind that developing a strong prayer life takes time and consistency. As you continue to pray and read the word, you will develop prayer stamina, endurance and vocabulary. Your prayer life will begin to increase and intensify. The strongest prayer warriors have been praying for years.

A few years ago, I took a special interest in running. I could only run for two minutes at a time. So, I would run two minutes and walk two minutes. I did this for weeks. Each week my running ability increased because I was consistent. The more I ran, the more empowered I became. I wanted to run longer and farther. I started researching how to endure when running. I also researched running shoes. I wanted to know what the best shoes were to run in. I began to invest in myself as a runner. I purchased the items I needed to become a good runner. I purchased fanny pacs, ear plugs for my music, running shoes, dry fit apparel, water bottles, running apps. I also began to eat differently. I drank a better quality of water. I did everything I could to grow. I was not concerned about speed, but I was concerned about endurance and perseverance.

Endurance is the ability to sustain a prolonged, stressful effort or activity.

Perseverance is continued effort to do or achieve something despite difficulties, failure or opposition.

To develop in prayer, you must take the same measures. Be consistent! Be patient with yourself. Build knowledge by studying prayer. Read scriptures pertaining to prayer. The Bible is full of stories that demonstrated how consistent and fervent prayers have manifested deliverance for entire nations, such as: Esther, Moses, Daniel, David and Nehemiah.

When you first start praying, your prayer will more than likely be short and sweet. Be okay with that! Little is better than nothing at all. Invest in things that help you develop your prayer life. Purchase books on prayer, prayer CDs, attend training and prayer conferences. Get a prayer partner. Be intentional about your development. Warning: There are a lot of books and teaching about prayer that are not of God. Before purchasing or reading anything, pray and ask God to lead you to resources that are Holy Spirit inspired. We must ensure that the writers, trainers or teachers present information that is according to the word of God. I highly advise you to research authors before purchasing books just to get an understanding of their faith and beliefs. Keep in mind that every religion has a firm belief in prayer, but they are not praying to the same God as we do. As believers of Jesus Christ, we pray to the one and only true and living God, the Creator of all of heaven and earth. He is the God who sacrificed His only begotten Son Jesus for all of mankind! Jesus was God in the flesh who came down and experienced an awful death because of His love for mankind. When He died, He rose on the third day with all power in His hands. He died not to save us from Satan but from the wrath of God. His death reconciled us back to God as His sons. Jesus, in his deity paid the price for our past, present and future sin. The only requirement is that we believe Jesus was the Son of God and He died for our sins. Any prayer teachings that are not derived from our foundational belief in Jesus Christ is probably not going to be aligned with the Bible. I highly suggest asking skilled prayer warriors for recommendations on what to read and always be led by the Spirit of God.

CHAPTER 5

PRAYER AND THE CONDITION
OF THE HEART

In order for us to be effective in prayer, we must understand that praying has nothing to do with how loud you pray, how fast or how eloquent. Believe it or not it has nothing to do with how many scriptures you quote. It's the condition of the heart that moves God! Man looks at the outward appearance of a thing, but God looks at the heart.

1 Samuel 16:7 (NKJV) "But the Lord said to Samuel, do not look at his appearance or at his physical stature, because I have refused him. For the Lord does not see as man sees, for man looks at the outward appearance, but the Lord looks at the heart."

Some can have the appearance that they are praying powerful, effective prayers, but if the condition of their heart is not right towards God and his people, their prayers can be ineffective. All prayers should be rooted in humility, faith and love for God and love for his people, both believers and non-believers. Our motives must be pure concerning prayer. God examines our heart. He's looking for people who are willing to pray according to His will and not their own. Jesus warns us in *Matthew 6:5-7 "And when thou prayest, thou shalt not be as the hypocrites are: for they love to pray standing in the synagogues and in the corners of the streets, that they may be seen of men. Verily I say unto you, They have their reward. But thou, when though prayest, enter into thy closet, and when thou hast shut thy door, pray to thy Father which is in secret; and thy Father which seeth in secret shall reward thee openly."* He warns us not to be hypocritical in our prayers. We should not pray, hoping to gain the attention of others. We do not have to impress God with our prayers. The believer should always examine his or her heart before praying. Ask God to remove all pride, anger, resentment, doubt, hatred or lack of forgiveness. Ask Him to remove anything that hinders you from effectively praying. Resist the temptation to be showy and theatrical in prayer, there is a difference. Fervency is derived out of real passion and zeal, but theatrics are dramatic performances which are artificial.

It's usually in corporate prayer that we feel the pressure to compete or impress others. Corporate prayer is when believers come together and pray out loud concerning various topics. It is very necessary, but it does not negate the believer's right to have a private prayer life with God. Pure love must be our motivation for prayer! We must pray from the very same heart Christ has. Some of our corporate prayer gatherings have become theatrical gatherings. They are filled with people in prayer shawls who attempt to impress each other with their loud and boisterous prayers. They have an appearance of Godliness, but deny the power thereof. We must be careful not to be one who appears righteous outwardly but inwardly we are full of dry bones and rotten fruit. Meaning our heart is unclean. Don't let your prayers become a performance.

I often hear people say that we should pray from our heart! I think this is great as long as we have a renewed heart. Let's examine the nature of the human heart. *Jeremiah 17:9 "The heart is deceitful above all things, and desperately wicked: who can know it?"* The human body is made up of three parts: soul, body and spirit. The soul consists of your emotions, mind, thoughts, personality and reasonings. The heart is part of the soul. The soul is what needs saving. The soul is what God is after. The soul/heart must be renewed daily by reading the word and the convictions of Holy Spirit. We must put on the new heart. The renewing of the heart and mind is a process, it takes time and effort and the work of the Holy Spirit. Some of our hearts are broken, wounded and full of toxic emotions. Sometimes, we have mess in our hearts that we don't realize exist.

Let me share a story about Ms. Jackson. Ms. Jackson was a powerful woman of God, full of Holy Spirit. When she opened her mouth to speak it was like God himself was speaking. Ms. Jackson went through a trial which caused her to lose everything; her home, cars, ministry and children. Ms. Jackson was also betrayed by someone close to her. As a result, she was full of hurt, anger, resentment, bitterness and unforgiveness. Her soul/heart just couldn't take anymore. One particular day, someone made her really angry. Out of her wounded soul, Ms. Jackson prayed and asked God to cause the person to lose everything. She wanted the person to experience everything she had gone through. Ms. Jackson's heart was full of toxic emotions, which caused her to pray from that place. Those prayers that she prayed was ineffective because it was not according to the word or will of God. She prayed witchcraft prayers opposed to Holy Spirit inspired prayers. The word of God tells us to love our enemies. We are to bless those who curse us and pray for those who despitefully use us. So, we must be careful when praying from the heart. If the heart is toxic, your prayers may be toxic and ineffective. As prayer warriors, we must guard our hearts or the very toxic nature will eventually exude out of your mouth. Guard against hatred, anger, malice, disunity, envy, jealousy, rebellion, stubbornness, gossip, lying and the likes. Keep your hearts pure by repenting daily, forgiving and turning all your worries, anxieties and frustrations over to Jesus. Ask God to create in you a clean heart and renew a right spirit within you. Your heart should be full of love, compassion, mercy, kindness, goodness, meekness, gentleness, humility, understanding and patience. These are the hearts that move God. These are the hearts that God can use to pray his will in the earth. God is looking for prayer warriors with a pure motive and a good heart. These are the hearts that produce effective prayers that manifest the promises of God. James 4:3 tells us that when we ask and do not receive, it's because our motives were wrong. We get caught up in what we want versus what God wants. If we take the time to find out what his will is, I guarantee we will see our prayers answered. It's written in *1 John 5:14 says; "This is the confidence we have in approaching God, that if we ask anything according to his will, he hears us."* And if we know that he hears us, whatever we ask, we know that we have received. He's not looking for a perfect heart, but a repented heart.

Here are some steps that can assist with guarding your heart:

- Ask Holy Spirit to help you examine your motives for prayer.
- Ask Holy Spirit to help you examine your heart.
- Repent of any unclean motives.
- Repent of any toxic emotions.
- Forgive those who hurt you.
- Ask God to help you guard your heart from toxic emotions.
- Ask God to help you pray his will and not your own.

CHAPTER 6

PRAY THE WORD

We've learned that if we want our prayers to be effective, we must pray with pure motives and a renewed heart. We've learned that we must pray the will of God. The question is; How do we know what the will of God is? The will of God can be discovered two ways, in his word and by his spirit. We need the knowledge of both operating in our lives. The Holy Bible is his word, which is his instructions and the Holy Spirit is the power which enables us to carry out those instructions. The word itself is God! *John 1:1 says; "In the beginning was the Word and the Word was with God, and the Word was God."*

If you want to know God, you must discover him in his word. If you want to know how he thinks, what he loves and what he hates, you must study his word. To know the mind of Christ means you know his word. If you want to pray effectively, we must know what he thinks concerning what you are praying about. As prayer warriors, we must be willing to forsake everything we've learned before accepting Jesus Christ. We must accept the word of God as our standard for living. Let's look at some of the reasons why praying the word of God yields results.

Prayer and the Word

• **Warfare:** As believers and followers of Jesus Christ, we are in a constant battle against the kingdom of darkness. It is God's will that we live a good life, filled with peace and harmony. However, the enemy violently fights against the plan of God for our lives. He attacks our mind, finances, families, health, churches, relationships and more. Our God, is not ignorant to the devices of Satan, neither has he left us ignorant to those devices (2 Corinthians 2:11 NLT). He has left us a mighty weapon, which equips us to overcome the plan of the enemy. He left his Word! The Apostle Paul in his letter to the Ephesians refers to the word of God as "the sword of the spirit." Prophet Jeremiah describes the word as: *"a mighty hammer that smashes a rock" Jeremiah 23:29 NLT.* When we pray, it is imperative that we pray the word of God. When we pray the word of God, it literally enforces God's will over the plans of the enemy. The word of God literally becomes a sword, cutting down spiritual strongholds. Praying the word brings light into darkness. We can't move God or Satan by praying our own thoughts or opinions. As human beings, our thoughts and opinions don't always line up with God's will or word, which will cause our prayers to lack power, effectiveness and go unanswered. God responds to his word!

- **Transformation:** As we pray and meditate on the word, we are literally opening our minds to be transformed. When our minds are transformed, we produce the fruit of Christian living (Romans 12:2). Meditate to keep the mind fixed on something good, pleasing and perfect.

- **Activating faith**: When we pray the word, we are reminding God of his promises. Make no mistake, God never forgets. He's fully aware of his word. He does not need us to remind him, but when we go to him, in the power of his word, he is faithful and obligated to respond to what he has spoken.

- **Humility:** Praying the word is an action that demonstrates true humility. One who prays the word recognizes that the answers are not in them. It's an example of the abandonment of self and placing trust in God's word and authority.

- **Hit the Bullseye:** Praying on target means praying the word. The word offers a solution to every problem. We don't pray the problem, we pray the solution!

No one can remember every scripture verbatim. It's okay to paraphrase and pray in alignment with scripture. It will be just as effective. However, every believer should make it a goal to memorize scriptures. Some find this to be a struggle. Start by trying to remember one scripture a week, before you know it, you will have a memory full of the word. The Bible tells us that Holy Spirit will bring all things to our remembrance, but we must give him something to work with. He can't bring anything to our remembrance if we never had it in our minds to start with. Load your mind with scriptures and when you need it in prayer, the Holy Spirit will bring the scriptures you need to your mind.

CHAPTER 7

PRAYER AND HOLY SPIRIT

God the Father is the Creator
God the Son is the Redeemer
God the Holy Spirit is the Maker of the New Creation

To pray effectively, we must be completely dependent on Holy Spirit to guide us in prayer. Our payers should always be Holy Spirit led. You can be sure that God will answer your prayers when you pray in tune with Holy Spirit. In this Chapter, we will explain who Holy Spirit is and His purpose.

Who is Holy Spirit? Holy Spirit is part of the trinity. We have God the Father, God the Son and God the Holy Spirit, all operating as one. We describe Holy Spirit as a person. Holy Spirit is a person! Holy Spirit has a personality, emotions and will. His will, just like Jesus' will, is to obey and enforce the will of the Father. Holy Spirit accomplishes what is on the mind of the Father. Holy Spirit is God's power in action. The Holy Spirit is a gift from God to believers. Jesus promised before he left that his spirit would be sent to live inside of believers.

How do we receive the Holy Spirit? We are sealed with the Holy Spirit the moment we hear and accept the message of the death, burial and resurrection of Jesus Christ. The Holy Spirit comes to dwell in us. Ephesians 1:13-14 tells us that every born-again believer has the spirit of God living on the inside of them. Our bodies are literally the temple of God. The

Holy Spirit is given to us for a number of reasons. Let's look at a few:

- **Teach:** To cause or help a person to learn how to do something by giving lessons, showing how it's done. The Holy Spirit is given to teach believers how to do whatever God needs us to do. God will never give us an assignment that he is not willing to prepare us for. Holy Spirit is the best teacher. He will teach you to pray. All you have to do is show up for prayer and open your mouth. Maintain your prayer posture! God has many anointed leaders on earth, but there are some things you will learn one on one with Holy Spirit. Rely on him as your teacher. He will use people, books, dreams, whatever he needs to get the job done.

- **Guide:** Someone or something who leads or directs other people on a journey. A person who helps direct another person's behavior. Holy Spirit will guide you in prayer. When in prayer he may guide you by bringing a particular person to your mind. When he does that, usually that is the unction to pray for that person. Always go into prayer with an open mind. I know we have our own prayer needs, but we should always ask God what to pray about. And he will respond. Let him guide you through your prayer. *John 16:13 "Holy Spirit will guide you into all truth."* Trust the Holy Spirit to show you what and who to pray for. You can't miss with his leading and guiding.

- **Empowers:** To make someone stronger and more confident. To give someone the authority or power to do something. Holy Spirit empowers us to pray. We become more confident in our prayer ability when we allow Holy Spirit to lead. By the empowering of the Holy Spirit we can pray with confidence, power, passion, faith and zeal, knowing that our prayers will be answered. As humans we are limited physically. We have so many responsibilities and things going on in our minds. We don't always know what people are going through, what's happening in the world or where prayer is needed most, unless Holy Spirit reveals it to us. 1 *Corinthians 2:10-12 says; "But God hath revealed them unto us by his Spirit for the Spirit searcheth all things, yea, the deep things of God. For what man knoweth the things of a man, save the spirit of man which is in him? Even so the things of God knoweth no man, but the Spirit of God. Now we have received, not the spirit of the world, but the spirit which is of God; that we might know the things that are freely given to us of God."*

We may not know all things, but God does and he will reveal to us what he wants us to know. We are one body connected by the same Spirit. The Spirit of God knows all of our issues and sometimes he will reveal to others just enough information so they can pray effectively for you. From the age of 23, I was in an abusive relationship. I suffered verbal and physical abuse for many years. I tried to hide it from my family. One day, I remember Grandma Emma calling me specifically asking me if everything was okay. I recall her telling me "I'm praying for you!" She was in-tune with Holy Spirit. She knew I needed prayer. She didn't have all the details, but Holy Spirit gave her the unction to keep me in prayer. The effectual, fervent prayers of the righteous avails much, they are effective. Eventually, I came out of that relationship and I found real love and happiness in God. I strongly believe my escaping that relationship was a result of Grandma's prayers. The will of God was for me to get out and the prayers spoken in the earth realm set the manifestation into action. There is one Spirit operating in all believers. The same Spirit empowers, corrects, teaches, guides and leads us all. The Spirit is interceding for us all. Don't feel pressured to have a lot of words to say. Don't be upset with yourself if you can't seem to find the right words to say. This is not a bad thing. The lack of words will teach you how to depend on the leading of Holy Spirit. Your lack of words allows you an opportunity to sit still and listen for God's voice and the unction of Holy Spirit.

"In the same way the spirit comes to us and helps us in our weakness. We don't know what prayer to offer or how to offer it as we should, but the spirit himself [knows our need and at the right time] intercedes on our behalf with sighs and groaning too deep for words. And he who searches the hearts knows what the mind of the spirit is, because the spirit intercedes (before God) on behalf of God's people in accordance with his will." (Romans 8:26-27 Amplified). When you don't know what to say, the Spirit will intervene. Notice in the scripture that the Spirit intercedes for God's people according to his will.

The manifestation of the Spirit praying through you can include: tears, speaking in tongues, crying out, moaning and groaning, that express emotions like sadness or joy.

Developing a prayer life which is Holy Spirit led can take some time. Why? Because our carnal mind is always at war against the Spirit. It can keep us from submitting to the instruction or prompting of the Spirit. Doubt, fear, uncertainty will set in. God is so amazing! God has been God since forever! He designed us. He knew that our carnal nature, (intellect, reasoning and logic) would war against his Spirit. So what he does, by way of the Holy Spirit, takes us through a process. As we humble ourselves, submit and come to him in prayer he will begin to train us. I like to call it "the school of Holy Spirit." We go through a trial and error process. We have to understand that God wants us to be successful in him. He wants us to grow. He's not going to tell us to pray according to his Spirit, operate by his Spirit and not teach us how to do it. He's wise! Many people will ask, "How do I know when Holy Spirit is speaking to me?" Holy Spirit speaks to people in different ways!

He speaks through:
- Dreams
- Open visions
- Visions or images in the mind
- Impressions
- His Word
- People
- Nature
- Knowings

Look for God in everything! Practice makes perfect!

The most important way he speaks is by his word. Holy Spirit will never contradict or go against God's word. It will always lead to God's will being done. The voice of Holy Spirit will point back to God, not self. One Sunday my pastor was praying for a young lady, Holy Spirit told him to pray against suicide. Holy Spirit knew what the issue was. He could have prayed about money, a spouse or kids, but he was led by Holy Spirit. Holy Spirit revealed what was on the mind of God concerning that young lady. We want to be careful to listen for the unction of the Holy Spirit also, not just to pray based on what we know about people or judge from outer appearance. It may not always make sense to you intellectually, but you must learn to trust Holy Spirit. If someone gives you something specific to pray for, pray that and if Holy Spirit gives you something else, pray it. Being led by the Spirit in prayer means dying to self in our prayer lives. We must submit to God!

Are you humble? Are you arrogant, prideful, full of self, or determined to do it your way? In order to be led by the Spirit, we must be open-minded to the Spirit; teachable, patient and consistent. Is your heart right? Can God trust you to pray for those who hurt you, who get on your nerves, who mistreat you? (Luke 22:32) When God wakes you up at three o'clock in the morning? Will you die to yourself and pray? Jesus was disheartened because the disciples couldn't stay awake for one hour. Are you the one? Will you be the gatekeeper for your family? Will you be the one who allows Holy Spirit to pray and intervene through you? All it takes is a yes!

CHAPTER 8

INTERCESSION

Many have asked the question; "Am I an intercessor?" Let's be clear, every believer is an intercessor. We all carry the same command to pray for one another. Intercession is the action of saying a prayer on behalf of others. An intercessor is someone who intervenes on behalf of someone else, especially in prayer. *James 5:16 "Therefore, confess your sins one to another and pray for one another, that you may be healed."* The prayer of a righteous person has great power. We all carry the responsibility to be our brother's keeper, especially in prayer.

God desires people who are willing to stand in the gap for others. He desires people to forget about themselves and be committed to the assignment of praying for their brothers and sisters. The world as we know is in such chaos. Our communities and nations are plagued with addictions, poverty, perversion, homosexuality, disunity, gossiping, slander, broken marriages, self-idolatry, witchcraft, new age spiritual practices and more. It's disheartening to admit this, but these very same issues are plaguing the church. The hearts of the people have been hardened. They refuse to repent and they have become dishonorable, rebellious, stubborn and unyielding. This grieves the heart of God. God wants nothing more than to have a relationship with his children. He wants a relationship that through love and admiration we become compelled to yield to his Spirit and obey him.

What grieves the heart of God should grieve his people. The burden of the current state of our communities and nation should grieve the believers. This grieving along with the love of God is what should cause us to intercede like never before. The problem is, many of us have become distracted by daily life. We've become consumed with me, myself and I! We also have spiritual forces fighting against our prayer lives. *Ephesians 6:12 says; "We wrestle not against flesh and blood, but against principalities, against powers, against the rulers of the darkness of this world. Against spiritual wickedness in high places."* Yes, there are demonic spirits assigned to hinder your prayer life. A major indication that you have a spirit fighting against your prayer life is if you fall asleep every time you start to pray or major distractions come up when you set your mind to pray. The enemy is aware of the impact your prayer will have in the earth realm. He wants to stop you from prospering in prayer. There is power in prayer! If you recognize that you may have a spirit fighting against your prayer life, do not be dismayed. Greater is He that's in you than he that is in the world. Pray and ask God to deliver you from the influence of every unclean spirit. Ask him to restore your prayer life. Ask him to give you a renewed zeal and passion for prayer and intercession. Call on the name of the Lord. He is sure to deliver!

God is calling us to stand in the gap and build the walls of our communities and nation through the vehicle of prayer. *Ezekiel 22:30 says; "And I sought for a man among them, that should make up the hedge, and stand in the gap before me for the land, that I should not destroy it: but I found none."* This word was spoken to the Prophet Ezekiel during a time when Israel was in a state of rebellion. The land was filled with idolatry, greed, disobedience to God's word, dishonesty, corrupt leaders and more. Does this remind you of something? This is the current state of the world we live in. And God is still the same God. He is still looking for people to stand in the gap and pray. Prayer is the way we rebuild the walls. Prayer is the way we manifest the will of God. We cannot afford to sleep or slumber during the times we should be praying. While we are sleeping, the enemy is still working around the clock (twenty-four-seven). His goal is to destroy our marriages and families by causing so much chaos until divorce is the only option. He wants to separate families by causing constant disagreement. He wants to get our children addicted to pornography, drugs, alcohol and prescription pills. He wants to rob us of our faith by alluring us into false religion. Intercessors are to watch and pray! We watch over our families, communities and nation. We discern what's happening within our sphere. We must seek God on how to pray and pray according to the word and Spirit of God. Intercessors are the front line of defense. We see attacks coming and we shoot them down with the word of God in prayer.

Prayer is how we fight in the Spirit. We don't fight our brother and sisters physically. We fight with prayer, love and faith. *"The weapons we use in our fight are not worldly weapons, but God's powerful weapons, which we use to destroy strongholds. We destroy false arguments"* 2 Corinthians 10:4 (GNT). The heart of the intercessor should be full of compassion which is a sympathetic pity and concern for the sufferings and misfortunes of others. Intercessors must refuse to harbor anger, resentment or unforgiveness toward people. Even if they hurt you, we must be quick to forgive. It's really hard to be compassionate towards someone when you have secret anger or haven't forgiven them in your heart. It is really hard to pray for people that you don't like or resent. Moses is a great example of a pure intercessor. Read Numbers 12. Grab your Bible now and go there. Read the entire Chapter.

Moses was described as a humble man. In fact, the scripture says he was the most humble man on earth. Moses' brother and sister talked against him and God punished the sister by striking her with leprosy. The carnal mind would have been happy to see those who talked against them punished, but Moses being an intercessor and a humble man of God, his heart was filled with compassion for her. He prayed to God on her behalf (interceded). He asked God to remove the wrath. There are several stories in the Bible where Moses prayed and pleaded with God on behalf of the children of Israel. The children of Israel often repaid him with murmuring and complaining. I'm sure Moses was tired of the people and got hurt at times but his desire to please God and the love for people caused him to persist in intercession.

We must answer the call and take our position as intercessors because the enemy is wreaking havoc in the earth. We must answer the call! Have you responded to the unction to pray for people or situations as the Holy Spirit placed them in your Spirit? Do you talk about them or murmur or complain? Make a decision today to pray for who and what is placed in your Spirit and watch God do the miraculous. Anything we ask according to his will He is faithful to perform.

PRAYER FOR INTERCESSORS

Father, in the Name of Jesus, I thank you for being God. I thank you for being a triune God. I give you praise for the Son and Holy Spirit. I ask today that you forgive me for not answering the call of intercession. Forgive me for not being in my prayer posture. Forgive me for allowing demonic forces to distract me from answering the call to pray and intercede. Forgive me for not praying for those who you have assigned to me or brought into my Spirit as an unction to cover them in prayer. I ask God that you renew and refresh my prayer life. Teach me discipline in prayer. Teach me how to pray your will and not my own. Teach me how to recognize when you are speaking to me. Remove any stones in my heart and give me a heart that is sensitive to the needs of your people and easily penetrated by your word and Holy Spirit. Help me to remain consistent. Remove all distractions in Jesus Name, I pray. Amen!

CHAPTER 9

THE POWER OF DECREEING AND DECLARING

When in prayer, we must make it a practice to declare and decree. People often use declare and decree in the same content, but they are quite different and both serves a different purpose. In order to declare and decree effectively, we must have a solid understanding of both words and scripturally understand why we declare and decree (the purpose).

Declare means to make known formally, officially or explicitly. When we "declare" we are simply making known what already is. When Jesus died on the cross he paid the price for our lives. He paid the price for our healing, deliverance and salvation. In His death and resurrection, He gave us power, authority and complete victory over the enemy. His death restored us back to right relationship with God. When we declare we are declaring the victories of what Jesus has already done for us. Your prayers should be filled with declarations of victory and triumph even when you can't see it! It may not look like you have the victory, but we know that you do because Christ has already given it to us.

I suggest you come up with a list of decrees for yourself and those you pray for. Recite them daily. When declaring, do it with boldness and confidence, know in your heart that what you are saying is so. Now that we have looked at declaring, let's look at decree!

Decree is an order usually having the force of law. A decree can only be given from someone who has authority to give it. There are two types of decrees; a royal decree and a judicial decree. As believers, we are part of a royal family. I already mentioned we were given authority and dominion through Jesus Christ. Every one of us have authority to make royal decrees. We must be careful to make decrees that are in line with Kingdom principle. Any decrees made outside of Kingdom principles will be ineffective. All decrees must line up with the Kings decree which is the word of God. When we operate in our authority and decree things in alignment with the word of God we will see manifestation. The scripture that sets the foundation for decreeing is *Matthew 6:6-10 "But thou, when thou prayest, enter into thy closet, and then thou hast shut thy door, pray to thy Father which is in secret; and thy Father which seeth in secret shall reward thee openly. But when we pray, use not vain repetitions, as the heathen do: for they think that they shall be heard for their much speaking. Be not ye therefore like unto them: for you Father knoweth what things ye have need of, before ye ask him. After this manner therefore pray ye: Our Father which art in heaven, Hallowed be thy name. Thy kingdom come, Thy will be done in earth, as it is in heaven."*

When decreeing, we are sending out an order for God's will to be done. A decree would usually be said for things that we are waiting on to manifest. For example: If a person is sick in the natural, as intercessors or prayer warriors, we would decree that person is healed. This decree is in line with scripture, because we know that Jesus paid the price so that we can be healed. Another example: If a couple is having marital problems and considering divorce, prayer warriors and intercessors have the authority to decree that the married couple will not divorce, but remain united as one. This decree is in line with scripture because the word of God tells us that man will leave his mother and father and become one with his wife.

I want you to pay attention to your language and what you speak! It makes no sense to declare and decree and then speak negative concerning your situation. If you are sick and you are praying and decreeing healing, refrain from statements like; "I will never get healed or I'm sick." You must continuously speak your healing. Stay away from people who speak contrary to what you are believing God for. Don't let your speech come into agreement with the plans of hell concerning your life or those around you. Let your speech line up to the Kingdom agenda for your life. Blessings and curses can't come out of the same mouth. If you are praying for your children and decreeing deliverance from rebellion, don't make statements like; "My child is bad or they get on my nerves." It's important to make statements that are contrary to their current issues. *The power of life and death is in the tongue (Proverbs 18:21)*. Always speak life! Many of us are praying and then wondering why we are not seeing change. Part of it is because the moment we get out of prayer we go back to speaking negatively concerning what we are praying about. Let's make a decision to speak life at all times. If you need to vent or confide in someone, ask God to lead you to a trusting person who can help you and join forces with you in prayer. Don't share your concerns with everybody you come across because they may not lead you in the right direction. You need someone full of wisdom and understanding and skilled in prayer.

SAMPLE DAILY DECLARATIONS

- I decree and declare that my entire body is healed.
- I decree and declare that my marriage/relationship is prosperous.
- I decree and declare all of my children are saved.
- I decree and declare that my finances are growing.
- I decree and declare that my mind is at peace.
- I decree and declare that my community is drug free.
- I decree and declare I have total victory
- I decree and declare I am delivered.
- I decree and declare I am an overcomer.
- I decree and declare I am blessed and favored.
- I decree and declare I walk in dominion, authority and power.
- I decree and declare generational curses and cycles are broken off my life.
- I decree and declare I am free from every form of bondage and oppression.

This is just a sample list. I suggest you come up with a list of declarations for yourself and those you pray for. Recite them daily!

CHAPTER 10

BINDING AND LOOSING

As a Kingdom Citizen we were given the authority to bind and loose. In order to effectively bind and loose we must understand binding and loosing. So often believers sit and wait for God to make things happen. We fail to realize that God has given us the authority and power to enforce His will here on earth. *Matthew 16:19 "And I will give you the keys of the kingdom of heaven. Whatever you bind on earth will be bound in heaven, whatever you loose on earth will be loosed in heaven."* This scripture indicates that we have been given keys. Keys are a means of gaining or preventing entrance, possession or control. We have keys to the Kingdom of heaven, which lets me know that we have access to heaven. The Kingdom of heaven is not a physical location, but it is a Spiritual Kingdom. It is the power of God and Jesus working in the world today. It is not in a church building or specific location. The Kingdom of heaven is God's rule and reign in the hearts of men. Those who believe are citizens of the Kingdom of heaven and we are under God's rule. There are benefits to being a kingdom citizen. One of the benefits is the ability to bind and loose. Let's look at what it means to bind and loose. Bind means to tie or fasten. Loose means to make free from restraint. When in prayer, we must be sure to use the principle of binding and loosing because God has given us the authority. Why let this precious ability go to waste?

Before binding and loosing we must know how to effectively use it. When binding, we are tying up and restraining anything that is contrary to God's word or will. In the natural, if we tie up anything it loses its power. It loses its ability to move. Let's use a criminal for example, when a criminal commits a crime and is convicted by the judicial system they are usually given a prison sentence. They are taken to a jail or state penitentiary and locked behind prison walls with no physical access to the rest of the world. One of the major reasons criminals are sentenced to prison is to ensure that they no longer commit crimes. Prison confinement is an attempt to bind (tie criminals from recking havoc in the earth). The same way the judicial system binds criminals through conviction and prison confinement is the same exact method we use as Kingdom Citizens to bind illegal, spiritual activity, which wreaks havoc on our families, communities, churches and nations.

As prayer warriors or intercessors we are to constantly watch the conditions of our world and examine our atmosphere. We take note of what's happening in our homes, marriages, schools, government, and nation. We use the Holy Spirit given discernment to access the spirits operating around us. Once you have watched, then you must determine what's happening that is contrary to God's will. For example: Over the last few years, I noticed an increase in divorce in my community. I started watching and listening to identify the root cause for the divorce. After some time of evaluating, I noticed that marriages were suffering because of three main reasons: poor communication, unforgiveness and the inability to remain faithful. In my prayer time, I took each topic and I began to bind some of the issues associated with each of these problems in marriages:

Poor Communication

- I bind lack of communication in the Name of Jesus.
- I bind ineffective communication in the Name of Jesus.
- I bind anger, resentment, hatred and frustration operating in marriages in the Name of Jesus.

Unforgiveness

- I bind secret hurt operating in marriages in the Name of Jesus.
- I bind unforgiveness operating in marriages in the Name of Jesus.
- I bind anger, resentment, hatred and disunity operating in marriages in the Name of Jesus.

Adultery

- I bind perversion and seduction operating against our marriages in the Name of Jesus.
- I bind lust operating in our marriages in the Name of Jesus.
- I bind sexual discontentment operating in our marriages in the Name of Jesus.

When we bind those things that are contrary to God's word, we can be sure that heaven is backing us. We have His word that whatever we bind on earth is bound in heaven. We may not see it, but remember God is working in the Spirit. He's responding to our words! When we bind those things that are contrary to God's word, the next step is to loose. We must replace whatever we bind by loosing God's will. The next step is to identify by the word and Spirit of God what we should release. Let's look at the examples below. Now that those illegal offenses have been bound through prayer from operating in marriages, let's see how to loose. The first step is to examine scripture to see what God says about marriage.

"And over all these virtues put on love, which bonds them together in perfect unity." Colossians 3:14

"Therefore a man shall leave his mother and father and hold fast to his wife, and they shall become one flesh." Genesis 2:24

"Therefore what God has put together let no one separate" Mark 10:9

"Love is patient, love is kind. It does not envy, it does not boast, it is not proud. It does not dishonor others, it is not self-seeking. It is not easily angered, it keeps no record of wrongs." 1 Corinthians 13:4-5

"Marriage should be honored by all, and the marriage bed kept pure, for God will judge the adulterer and all the sexually immoral." Hebrews 13:4

After reading and meditating on these scriptures, I realized what I needed to loose in the marriages I was praying for. I took the same three issues and after binding, I loosed the opposite of what I had to bind.

Poor Communication

- I loose honor and respect in marital communication in the Name of Jesus.

- I loose edification and exhortation in marital communication in the Name of Jesus.

- I loose delight and pleasure in marital communication in the Name of Jesus.

- I loose peace, unity, understanding and harmony in our marriages in the Name of Jesus.

Lack of Forgiveness

- I loose forgiveness in marriages in the Name of Jesus.

- I loose unconditional love in our marriages in the Name of Jesus.

- I loose healing in our marriages in the Name of Jesus.

- I loose long-suffering and patience in the Name of Jesus.

Adultery

- I loose purity in our marriage bed in the Name of Jesus.

- I loose romantic passion back into our marriages in the Name of Jesus.

- I loose creative romance into our marriages in the Name of Jesus.

- I loose refreshing, joy, humor, fun and excitement back into our marriages in the Name of Jesus.

Binding and loosing is a strategic method of prayer. As believers we should be empowered to bind and loose. Jesus gave us permission in the written word of God. Binding and loosing is an effective way of praying in your authority. Just be sure when binding or loosing you are operating within the word and will of God. Find scriptures for your prayer targets that can help guide you on what to bind and loose. Allow the Holy Spirit to lead you throughout the process. Remember, a sure way to know you are praying God's will is to find it through His word. If you are really new to the Kingdom you can google scriptures concerning whatever your prayer topic is. You can also turn to the back of your Bible and look in the concordance to find scriptures concerning your prayer topics. Feel free to use the same binding and loosing statements every day until you see results. You don't need a lot of words or statements. As you grow in confidence and prayer and study the scriptures, you will begin to flow and grow in binding and loosing. It will become a normal part of your daily prayer life. It will become natural and come with ease. As you develop, you will notice things happening outside of God's will and by prompting of Holy Spirit, you will immediately begin to bind and loose. Holy Spirit will assist by bringing the appropriate scriptures and words to your memory.

CHAPTER 11

PRAYER AND FAITH

"The centurion answered and said, Lord, I am not worthy that thou shouldest come under my roof: but speak the word only, and my servant shall be healed. For I am a man under authority, having soldiers under me: and I say to this man, Go, and he goeth; and to another, Come, and he cometh; and to my servant, Do this, and he doeth it. When Jesus heard it, he marvelled, and said to them that followed, Verily I say unto you, I have not found so great faith, no, not in Israel." Matthew 8:8-10

All prayer should be done in faith. Faith is complete confidence or trust in something or someone. Our faith should not be in other humans or ourselves, instead our faith should be in God. Other humans will fail us and we will disappoint ourselves, but God will never fail us! We can have complete trust and confidence that all of His promises will come to pass. Unlike many, God cannot and will not lie. The only requirement to being adopted into the Kingdom of Heaven is that we have faith. We must believe in God and Jesus Christ as the Son of God. Faith is a prerequisite for the believer. Faith is so important to God. Without faith it is impossible to please Him. *Hebrews 11:6 "But without faith it is impossible to please him; for he that cometh to God must believe that he is and that he is a rewarder of them that diligently seek him."* As prayer warriors we must develop the *Ephesians 3:20* mentality. *"Now to him who is able to do exceedingly, abundantly more than we could ask or think."* We must take on the mindset that says; "God can do all things!" We must remind ourselves that God's promises are already fulfilled. As prayer warriors we are simply praying the promises by faith. As prayer warriors, it is imperative that we do not get distracted by what our situations look like in the natural. We must be determined to walk by faith and not by sight. God is always working, even when we can't physically see change. Remember that God's work is always done in the inside of man's heart before it manifests outwardly.

Let me give you an example. When I was believing God for my husbands' salvation, I would hear God clearly say; "I'm working on his heart." When I heard his words, I would fall to my knees and cry. My face would be filled with tears, my heart flooded with joy. I would give God an exuberant praise! When I received the word of God, it seemed like the moment I left prayer, my husband would do something that would be a direct contradiction to what God just spoke to me. I would come out of prayer and the whole house would reek of marijuana or we would have a huge argument. As a result of these natural manifestations, I would question if my prayers were working or if I really heard God concerning my husband's salvation. I wondered were my prayers effective. It caused me to doubt God. The mistake I made was that I got caught up in what things looked like in the natural. All God wanted from me was to walk in love, keep praying and keep believing that he would do it. I know that I'm not alone. Many get distracted by the appearance of things and we stop praying in faith. We stop hoping and we lose expectations. Perhaps you are praying for your marriage or your children. Maybe you are praying for your unsaved friends and family to get saved. Some are praying for financial breakthrough or physical healing. Whatever you are praying for it is going to take relentless faith and prayer. I encourage you not to get weary. Don't lose faith or hope. Keep believing! It is faith that moves God! Keep declaring and decreeing by faith. Pray and ask God to increase your faith in Him. Faith is the key to persistent prayer. Faith is the key to releasing your miracle. Jesus performed many miracles in the Bible. Let's examine. *Matthew 8:5-13 "And when Jesus was entered into Capernaum, there came unto him a centurion, beseeching him, And saying, Lord, my servant lieth at home sick of the palsy, grievously tormented. And Jesus saith unto him, I will come and heal him. The centurion answered and said, Lord, I am not worthy that thou shouldest come under my roof: but speak the word only, and my servant shall be healed. For I am a man under authority, having soldiers under me: and I say to this man, Go, and he goeth; and to another, Come, and he cometh; and to my servant, Do this, and he doeth it. When Jesus heard it, he marveled, and said to them that followed, Verily I say unto you, I have not found so great faith, no, not in Israel. And I say unto you, That many shall come from the east and west, and shall sit down with Abraham, and Isaac, and Jacob, in the kingdom of heaven. But the children of the kingdom shall be cast out into outer darkness: there shall be weeping and gnashing of teeth. And Jesus said unto the centurion, Go thy way; and as thou hast believed, so be it done unto thee. And his servant was healed in the selfsame hour."*

We can take some lessons from the centurion. He knew how to touch the heart of Jesus. He had the E320 mindset. GOD IS ABLE! Let's look at how he received his miracle from Jesus.

1. He recognized who Jesus was. He recognized Him as the Messiah.

2. He asked for help. He was honest with Jesus about his problems.

3. He humbled himself, recognizing that the power to heal his servant was not in him, but in Jesus.

4. He submitted his authority to Jesus. He recognized that he was a man of authority, but he honored Jesus as one greater than him. He edified Jesus as a higher authority.

5. He had faith in the power of Jesus and believed it could be done. He believed in the power of His word. He did not doubt His ability to heal.

Notice, the centurion was not believing for himself, but his servant. He went to Jesus on behalf of someone else. He had faith to believe God for another person's miracles. As prayer warriors and intercessors, we must have faith for everyone around us. We must boldly and confidently stand in the gap and believe God for miracles for our families, communities, nation, government and churches. We must believe for others when they can't believe God for themselves. As a result of the centurion faith, his servant was healed. The centurion and his servant received great victory. As you persist in prayer by faith, you too will see the manifestation of these types of victories. God's heart yearns for the day when men will pray simply because they believe. Faith says; "I know God has already promised us these victories, I will pray until we receive a manifestation." Faith says; "I won't give up in prayer until something happens." Faith moves God!

CHAPTER 12

THE LORD'S PRAYER

When speaking with believers who struggle with prayer, one of the top concerns I hear is; "I don't know how to pray." This is very disheartening to me. People have become stagnant in prayer because they have been persuaded that there is a certain formula that is used in prayer in order to reach God. As you travel through the Bible, you will notice several types of prayers. There is a prayer of supplication, prayer of thanksgiving, prayer of repentance and forgiveness, intercession, communion and prayers of agreement.

Prayer of Supplication - The prayer of supplication is presenting our needs to God. We should tell him daily what we need. He delights in giving us the desires of our hearts. (Philippians 4:6 Mathew 7:7; Mathew 6:11; Ephesians 6:18)

Prayer of Thanksgiving - Our hearts should be filled with thanksgiving to Abba. We should find every opportunity to give Him praise. Throughout our days, we should proclaim his goodness. Sometimes we should fill our prayers with praise and nothing else. We should pray without asking him for anything, just meditating on his love should be enough to usher us into a prayer of thanksgiving. (Psalm 116:17; Psalm 34; Psalm 86:12)

Intercession - The prayer of intercession is the act of praying for others. We should pray for the needs of those around us and pray for their wellbeing and protection. Intercession is a selfless act and should be done in love. (Nehemiah 1:4-11; James 5:14-16; 1 Samuel 12:19)

Prayer of Communion - The prayer of communion is the act of staying in fellowship with God all the time. It's a simple conversation with God; in the car, on the bus, at work, or while at home. It's the intentional practice of yielding, obeying, speaking and hearing from God. (2 Corinthians 13:14; 1 Corinthians 1:9)

Prayers of Agreement - The prayer of agreement is when two or more believers come together in agreement on various topics. These types of prayers can be done in corporate prayer gatherings with other believers or with prayer partners, friends or family members. (Matthew 18:19; 2 Chronicles 7:14)

Prayer of Repentance - The prayer of repentance is prayer that involves a time of self-examination and repentance from wrong doing. It's a time of prayer where we allow God to show us the error of our ways. We humbly receive his grace, mercy and forgiveness. It's a time of brokenness, cleansing and refreshing. (Matthew 4:17; Matthew 3:8; Acts 11:18; Jeremiah 31:19 2 2Chronicles 7:14)

We should consider the type of prayer we need to pray based on our individual circumstances. For example, a person who has been struggling with drug addiction and has been convicted by the Holy Spirit, should pray the prayer of repentance. The person struggling with the addiction would spend this time repenting for the wrong and asking God to forgive them as well as deliver them. The prayer of repentance would put them back in right standing with God. It will give them strength to continue on their journey. After repentance, the person should rest in God's mercy and forgiveness. This could also be followed with thanksgiving to God for forgiveness and a fresh start. Although there are many types of prayers, God's focus is more on your willingness to pray instead of a repetitious formula to pray. Matthew 6:7-13 gives us a clear view of how God feels about the purity and simplicity of prayer.

Matthew 6:7-13 (MSG)

"The world is full of so-called prayer warriors who are prayer-ignorant. They're full of formulas and programs and advice, peddling techniques for getting what you want from God. Don't fall for that nonsense. This is your Father you are dealing with, and he knows better than you what you need. With a God like this loving you, you can pray very simply. Like this: Our Father in heaven, Reveal who you are. Set the world right; Do what's best — as above, so below. Keep us alive with three square meals. Keep us forgiven with you and forgiving others. Keep us safe from ourselves and the Devil. You're in charge! You can do anything you want! You're ablaze in beauty! Yes. Yes. Yes."

God knows what we need before we ask. Even if we did miss the right words. The Spirit of God will intercede for us. He knows what the heart is saying even when we don't have the right words. Jesus does not want us getting distracted or stagnated by how we should pray. He left us with an example to help us.

This is our road map to help us navigate through prayer, but it is not the only way we can pray. I would like to erase the myth that if you do not say this exact prayer that God will not hear you. As you can see in the Bible, there were many types of prayers and He answered the cries of his people. (Psalms 51; 1 Kings 8: 22-61)

The Lord's prayer in Matthew 6 is an example of how we should navigate through prayer. This prayer is a general outline that teaches us the basics of what and how to pray.

After this manner therefore pray ye: Our Father which art in heaven, Hallowed be thy name.

10 Thy kingdom come, Thy will be done in earth, as it is in heaven.

11 Give us this day our daily bread.

12 And forgive us our debts, as we forgive our debtors.

13 And lead us not into temptation, but deliver us from evil: For thine is the kingdom, and the power, and the glory, for ever. Amen.

Let's break down this scripture a bit further.

Our father which art in heaven - Praying straight to God, not to the virgin Mary, not to angels, not to your dead loved ones (familiar spirit or necromancy) 1 Samuel 28; Forbidden in Leviticus 19:31; 20:6,

Deuteronomy 18:9-14. Consulting with the dead is an abomination to God and was forbidden. Prayers go to God through the Name of Jesus Christ. He is the only mediator between us and God.

Hallowed be thy name - We must honor his holiness and reverence his name, praying in humility.

Thy Kingdom come, thy will be done on earth as it is in heaven - A kingdom is a nation that is ruled by a monarch. A monarch is a king or queen. England is a monarch and queen Elizabeth II is the ruler. They have a set way of life in England that all must live by. There is an authority structure and a system set up with laws to ensure that everyone is living according to the standard of the kingdom. On earth, Satan is the prince of the power of the air. He rules here by his power and influence. We all were once under the influence before salvation. Once we accept Christ as our personal Lord and Savior, we are no longer a part of the kingdom of darkness. We are now Kingdom Citizens. We live according to a new system. We live under the influence of the Kingdom of heaven. It's a spiritual kingdom. It is God's rule and reign in the hearts of believers. We are to pray that his will is done in the earth realm. In other-words, whatever God wants is what we want to happen. That's what we are to pray for.

Give us this day our daily bread - We must recognize that he is the one who provides for us. The Bible says to ask him for what we need. We should demonstrate our faith by asking him to meet our need.

And forgive us our debts as we forgive our debtors -
It is he who forgives through the shed blood of Jesus
Christ. It's important to maintain a repentant heart. We
must have a daily prayer of repentance. As we forgive
our debtors - Believers and followers of Jesus Christ
cannot harbor unforgiveness. It blocks our prayers.
God won't forgive us. Read Matthew 18:21-35. We
want to have hearts full of love and compassion, quick
to forgive. Pray to forgive others quickly!

**And lead us not into temptation, but deliver us from
evil** - As Christians we will deal with temptation, but
we must consistently call on God to help us out. The
Bible says that he who calls on the name of the Lord
shall be saved. When we are tempted, He will provide
a way of escape. He will help you to endure. Pray for
God to give you strength over temptation.

**For thine is the Kingdom, the power and glory
forever and ever**. Amen – This seals the prayer.
Reinforcing the fact that God's Kingdom and will is
what is most important.

CHAPTER 13

PRAYING AND FASTING

Prayer coupled with fasting is an added bonus in prayer. Fasting and prayer when done properly has great value and pleases the heart of God. Fasting, like prayer is a must for believers. It is important that prayer warriors develop a disciplined life of fasting and praying. Fasting is the discipline of sustaining from all or some forms of food and drink for a specific period of time to seek the face of God.

Fasting is a phenomenon and is done by many religions. Fasting has a great number of benefits, therefore it has also become a recommended practice by doctors for their patients with various diseases such as diabetes, high blood pressure, obesity, heart disease, and the likes. Fasting has been proven to help the body heal and detoxify. It also assists with weight loss and weight management. It cleanses the digestive system, ridding the body of old toxins, which leads to increased energy and mental clarity. With all these benefits, who wouldn't want to fast!

Fasting can be done for various reasons. As believers when we set to fast, it should be to get closer to God. Let me be clear, anyone can fast for the physical benefits when needed, but the fast that is spoken of in the Bible helped get them closer to God. The physical benefits such as healing, weight loss, increased energy, mental clarity and the likes are all added benefits of fasting but the goal is to seek the face of God.

Fasting should be birthed out of a desperation to get closer to God. It says to God; "I need you more than anything." *Matthew 4:4 "But he answered and said it is written, man shall not live off of bread alone, but by every word that proceeds out of the mouth of God."* Just as natural food is necessary for our physical bodies, God's word is the food that is needed for our spiritual man. Fasting replaces natural meals with the word of God which is our spiritual food. When fasting, the believer refrains from food, but replaces the time they would usually spend eating with reading the word of God, meditating on the word and praying.

Breakfast - would be replaced with reading and praying.

Lunch - instead of going to the break room, you may sit at your desk or find a quiet place in the park to read and pray.

Dinner - Instead of dining at the table with the family, excuse yourself and go in your room and read and pray.

In doing this, you are showing God how much you desire Him! Fasting is not a way to manipulate God to get what you want, but it is a way of desperately calling on Him, seeking Him for guidance, clarity, strength, relationship and breakthrough.

You can't fast and ask God for a million dollars and bam, it appears, but if you need financial increase you can take a time of fasting and praying to seek God diligently concerning your finances. Fasting should be a time of closing out all outside voices, television, cell phones, social media and all other distractions. If you are fasting for financial gain, take your time with God and ask Him to deliver you from any form of financial ignorance, negligence, overspending, selfishness or lack of discipline. Ask God to teach you to sow and give willingly with a cheerful heart. Ask him to teach you how to apply His word concerning finances over your life. Ask him to give you an obedient Spirit. During your time of fasting, God will show you why you are over spending. He will reveal the areas where you need to do better. He will give you strategies for increase. For some, we spend money on material things because our hearts are connected to the things of this world. The Bible says where your treasure is your heart is there also (Matthew 6:21). Fasting will help starve cravings from worldly riches. It will crucify the flesh and help you gain discipline. So instead of receiving or buying things during your fast, God may tell you to give some items away or sow into someone's life. This will kill selfishness and greed operating within us. Take time to do for others. Visit the sick, pray for others, spend time with the elderly, serve someone else.

Fasting is more about God dealing with what's in the heart. A fast should be strategic and well planned. A fast is not just about turning down food. We must be careful not to let our fast become religious, meaning we fast out of obligation and tradition, but inwardly we are like dead bones. We should fast with a pure heart and with others in mind. We should remember to love our neighbors. We must treat others as we would like to be treated. Fasting out of tradition and obligation, but lacking love will be displeasing to God. Therefore, when we make the decision to fast, we must start with repentance of sins and our hearts' conditions, things we know or things we don't know are in our hearts. God warns us against fasting that displeases Him. *Isaiah 58 (MSG) says; "Shout! A full-throated shout! Hold nothing back—a trumpet-blast shout! Tell my people what's wrong with their lives, face my family Jacob with their sins! They're busy, busy, busy at worship, and love studying all about me. To all appearances they're a nation of right-living people—law-abiding, God-honoring. They ask me, 'What's the right thing to do?' and love having me on their side. But they also complain, 'Why do we fast and you don't look our way? Why do we humble ourselves and you don't even notice?' "Well, here's why: "The bottom line on your 'fast days' is profit. You drive your employees much too hard. You fast, but at the same time you bicker and fight. You fast, but you swing a mean fist. The kind of fasting you do won't get your prayers off the ground. Do you think this is the kind of fast day I'm after: a day to show off humility? To put on a pious long face and parade around solemnly in black? Do you call that fasting, a fast day that I, God, would like? "This is the kind of fast day I'm after: to break the chains of injustice, get rid of exploitation in the workplace, free the oppressed, cancel debts. What I'm interested in seeing you do is: sharing your food with the hungry, inviting the homeless poor into your homes, putting clothes on the shivering ill-clad, being available to your own families. Do this and the lights will turn on, and your lives will turn around at once. Your righteousness will pave your way. The God of glory will secure your passage. Then when you pray, God will answer. You'll call out for help and I'll say, 'Here I am.' "If you get rid of unfair practices, quit blaming victims, quit gossiping about other people's sins, If you are generous with the hungry and start giving yourselves to the down-and-out, Your lives will begin to glow in the darkness, your shadowed lives will be bathed in sunlight. I will always show you where to go. I'll give you a full life in the emptiest of places— firm muscles, strong bones. You'll be like a well-watered garden, a gurgling spring that never runs dry. You'll use the old rubble of past lives to build anew, rebuild the foundations from out of your past. You'll be known as those who can fix anything restore old ruins, rebuild and renovate, make the community livable again. "If you watch your step on the Sabbath and don't use my holy day for personal advantage, If you treat the Sabbath as a day of joy, God's holy day as a celebration, If you honor it by refusing 'business as usual,' making money, running here and there—Then you'll be free to enjoy God! Oh, I'll make you ride high and soar above it all. I'll make you feast on the inheritance of your ancestor Jacob." Yes! God says so!"*

If you align your fasting with God's word, you will experience cleansing, refreshing, clarity and breakthrough. When fasting, remember to keep it private. You do not need to boast about fasting for the attention of men. In fact, God warns us in *Matthew 6:18; "That thou appear not unto men to fast, but unto thy Father which is in secret: and thy Father, which seeth in secret, shall reward thee openly."*

A fast should be between you and God and those that need to know. I told my husband and children when I decided to take on a fast. My husband needed to know in case something went wrong medically and my children were always concerned when they saw that I was not eating. So, to ensure the peace and unity in my home and to allow my family the opportunity to pray for me during my fast, I always told them when I was fasting. It demonstrates unity in the household. Your spouse needs to be in prayer for your strength as well as watching. Fasting affects your energy, mood, mind and even hygiene (bad breath). It could affect your ability to cook, clean, drive, think and perform marital duties, especially in the first few days. Sometimes the family also is affected by way of the food. The food that would usually be cooked for your family may change because the family member that's fasting can't indulge.

The benefits combined with prayer are so great, the enemy will usually war against you when fasting. Strange things will sometimes happen. When these things happens don't be alarmed. Continue on until the end.

Examples:
- Unusual phone calls (especially from an ex)
- Sickness
- Flat Tires
- Family Issues (just fussing for no reason, school calling)

We should always keep a good physical appearance. Don't let yourself look run down. Let your appearance remain the same as it would if you were not fasting, when it remains between us and God. He will reward

us publicly for what we do privately. You will receive a reward from God that man can't give. For those who fast to be seen by others, they will not receive God's reward.
There are several types of fasts in the Bible.

- 40-Day fast - Jesus partook of a 40 day fast
- 3-Day fast - known as Esther's fast
- 21-Day fast - known as the Daniel fast
- Partial Fast (7-day, 1 day)

Study each fast and the results of each.

40-day Fast: Jesus partook in a 40-day fast. This fast should only be taken with doctor's approval and when led by the Holy Spirit. Jesus went without food and drink. It is not recommended to fast without water. Jesus overcame Satan's temptation on this fast. Mathew 4:1 Exodus 34:28

21-Day Fast: Eat no meat, no sweets and no bread. Drink water and Juice. Eat fruits and vegetables. The Prophet David did this fast when he was seeking God for an interpretation of a dream. He needed clarity from God. God provided clarity because of his fasting and praying. Daniel 10:2-3

Partial Fast: You can choose the hours of this fast (6am-6pm) or sun up to sun down are the most popular hours you can do a partial fast. 2 Samuel 1:12

3-Day Fast: Commonly known as an Esther Fast. This fast can be a full fast or a Daniel fast. Esther went on a

3-day fast when her people were about to lose their lives. She called for a corporate prayer and fasting and God delivered them. Because of her fasting and praying, a whole nation of people was saved from the hands of their enemies. Esther 4:16

Scriptures for fasting, prayer and reading the word:

- 1 Samuel 1:6-8; 17-18
- Nehemiah 1:4
- Daniel 9:3
- Joel 2:12
- Luke 2:37
- Acts 10:30
- Acts 13:2
- Matthew 9:14-15
- Luke 18:9-19

If you're experiencing health issues, you can fast for one day and God would be pleased. He knows all things. He knows what you are capable of. One day or three hours of fasting is better than no fasting at all. Ultimately, the times and length of your fast is between you and God. Remember, fasting is about the attitude of the heart, sincerely seeking God. When our heart sincerely seeks after God, He will respond with blessings. He will give you exactly what you need!

PLANNING YOUR FAST

Strategic plan: To start anything without a plan is to set yourself up for failure. Why? You have no clear focus, no point of destination, no goal, no map. The plan is like the map to help you reach your destination. Businesses, major corporations, small business, all must develop a plan. Therefore, they do a vision statement, mission statement, business plan, financial plan, rules of conduct, code of ethics, etc. This is what they live by to accomplish their goals. When fasting, a plan is necessary!

- Determine the purpose of your fast.

- Develop a plan (write it down so you may understand it). No scribble, scrabble. I've had things I wrote down and come back and can't understand it. Make it plain, make sure it's doable and attainable. Don't write you're going to get up at three o'clock in the morning during the fast for prayer and you know you can't even get up at nine o'clock. I remember when I first started fasting and praying, I would set my alarm clock for three o'clock every morning, but I would shut it off. Why? Because it was not possible for me. It was unrealistic. I was still struggling to get up at seven o'clock. So, I decided to set a more realistic goal and stick to six o'clock, this worked a lot better. I was consistent. Be realistic in planning.

- Prepare and purchase food ahead of time. Don't go on a 21-day fast and you know you don't have money for the food you need. You will fail. Prepare your meals.

- Identify and avoid distractions - phone calls, mute phones, leave the television off, don't sit in the break room at work.

- See it through until the end. Hold onto it like a pit-bull hold onto a bone.

- If you do mess up, don't quit! Get back on track! Ask someone close to you to hold you accountable. Don't go to the places where you know you will be tempted to cheat.

- Celebrate your completion. Remember the longer the fast, the lighter your meals must be when transitioning from a fast. Your digestive system has been cleansed. For instance, if you choose a 21-day fast, your digestive system will become accustomed to digesting whole foods not processed foods. Processed food takes longer to digest and causes your digestive system to work harder. So your system is not ready to break down processed foods after a 21-day fast. You must ease back in slowly. So, a big juicy steak may not be the best celebration meal. Try a piece of salmon and a salad and work yourself back to your normal way of eating or you can start eating healthy and reap the benefits. Either way, celebrate your success!

- Buy a journal and journal what you learn and hear throughout the fast.

CHAPTER 14

PRAY WITHOUT CEASING

I have strategically placed this Chapter at the end. The Bible instructs us to **pray without ceasing.** We now understand that prayer is a conversation with God. The word 'cease' means to put a stop or end to. It means to discontinue. If we put the two definitions together it means to pray and don't stop or don't stop praying. In this day and time, it's very hard to imagine praying without stopping. When we hear this term, we often think of sitting in a room on our knees and praying all day and all night. If this is what the scripture meant, I think many of us would be disqualified from being prayer warriors. This instruction can be applied two ways:

First, to pray without ceasing or pray and don't stop is to simply talk to God throughout your day. It means whenever problems arise, the first person you talk to should be God. It means when something great happens, the first person you talk to should be God. Pray without stopping means you look for God in every situation. If you are in a restaurant having dinner and your waitress seems to be having a tough day, in that moment you can sit at your table and pray for them without anyone knowing but you and God. Perhaps you are driving in your car and you notice an accident on the side of the road. Right from your vehicle in passing, you can say a prayer for the people involved in the accident. Prayer without ceasing is having a spirit of prayer by remaining in communion with God and being sensitive to Holy Spirit's unction to pray. A person who prays without ceasing develops a strong relationship with Holy Spirit and is a yielded vessel to pray when needed. This does not have to be deep and spooky, you don't have to make a scene or let anyone else know that you are praying. It is literally between you and the Father.

The second aspect of praying without ceasing is described in *Luke 11:5-13 "And he said unto them, Which of you shall have a friend, and shall go unto him at midnight, and say unto him, Friend, lend me three loaves; For a friend of mine in his journey is come to me, and I have nothing to set before him? And he from within shall answer and say, Trouble me not: the door is now shut, and my children are with me in bed; I cannot rise and give thee. I say unto you, Though he will not rise and give him, because he is his friend, yet because of his importunity he will rise and give him as many as he needeth. And I say unto you, Ask, and it shall be given you; seek, and ye shall find; knock, and it shall be opened unto you. For every one that asketh receiveth; and he that seeketh findeth; and to him that knocketh it shall be opened. If a son shall ask bread of any of you that is a father, will he give him a stone? or if he ask a fish, will he for a fish give him a serpent? Or if he shall ask an egg, will he offer him a scorpion? If ye then, being evil, know how to give good gifts unto your children: how much more shall your heavenly Father give the Holy Spirit to them that ask him?"* In this text, God uses a metaphor to describe relentless prayer. He uses the example of a person who goes to their friend's house in the middle of the night to ask for food for their guest. He states that the friend would probably reject you and tell you to get away. It's not the fact that you are friends that will cause the person to give, but it's the boldness and relentless asking that will cause the person to give. Jesus uses this parable to admonish believers to keep asking God for what they want. He's encouraging them to never stop praying. He's saying if it looks like it's impossible keep asking your Father. Your persistence can produce a breakthrough and manifest answered prayers.

The Bible instructs us not to get weary in well doing because in due season we will reap a harvest. When you pray without ceasing, imagine yourself in a delivery room getting ready to give birth to a child. For men, let's imagine you in the room with your wife and she's on the table getting ready to deliver. It's time to push! In prayer you are literally birthing things in the spirit realm. You are on the delivery table pushing in prayer until the manifestation of the prayer breaks through.

Usually the first part of the delivery is really hard. When the woman initially prepares to give birth there is no manifestation of the baby. It's just pain, she's having contractions. When we first begin to pray for breakthrough in various areas of our lives, we usually don't see breakthrough, but we are in pain. We are disheartened by the situation of those around us. We are frustrated, we become anxious for change and as we pray we grow weary and faint. We are tempted to stop praying because we are tired of waiting. When a woman is in childbirth she gets to the place of wanting to stop pushing several times before birth, but her coaches in the room, the doctors and family encourages and coaches her to continue to push. So with everything she has she pushes. She's tired, she's weak, but she understands the importance of delivering her baby. So it is in prayer, when we grow weary, the Holy Spirit, our coach will pull and tug on us to continue to pray. He will remind us that the breakthrough is almost there. He may send a prophetic word from a prophet, we may have a vision or dream or perhaps he will give us a scripture that lets us know that we are close to change and not to give up. The woman in childbirth will push through with the help of her coaches until she finally pushes to the point where she receives her breakthrough, the head starts to crown. She's feeling the pain but relieved because she's seeing the progress and she's almost there. The prayer warrior, with the help of Holy Spirit should continue to push and eventually you will see the crowning of your breakthrough, you may feel the pain of labor from the process, but you're now close to the promise. Keep praying! Slowly you will see change, slowly you will see God moving, slowing with every push the promise is coming forth. Just because you see change, don't stop praying until the full manifestation of what you are praying for comes forth. The woman in labor is not done pushing until the baby is fully out of the womb. Then and only then is her task complete. Prayer warriors, pray until you see manifestation, don't give up. It may take days or it can take years. Hang in there! If God has given you someone or something to pray for, stay with your assignment. Don't stop praying! And when in labor, remember to breathe! Breathing is trusting in his promise, breathing is taking time to enjoy your life. Breathing is trusting that God is able and refusing to worry about anything. Breathing is eating your favorite food or reading a good book. In the labor room, the woman in labor is allowed to take a few moments between pushing to rest. Prayer warriors, you must take time to rest! Remember praying without ceasing is not a job to dread. It's a lifestyle of partnering with God and praying in our own unique way. Praying is a time of refreshing. It should not be hard, but delightful. There are enemies that want to rob you of a delightful prayer life, but we will delight ourselves in God. Yes, there will be some hard days when you are tired and don't want to pray. If you are tired, say thank you Abba and rest, breathe! Just don't let it become a habit. God is not in heaven keeping count of how many times you missed prayer time. Just don't make it a habit and completely stop praying, fight to keep your prayer life growing and consistent. For some, you may be the only one they have praying for them. And your prayer life will cause growth, strength and maturity in God.

Lastly, allow me to leave this with you! After you have prayed God's will in faith, and did everything you know to do in prayer, trust God no matter what happens in life. We will have some disappointments, we will have some hurts, we will experience some setbacks in life. It's important that we understand that all things work together for the good of those who love God. The word didn't say that good things work together for our good, but it says, **all** things work together for our good. We don't have all the answers to why we have natural disasters or why the young die early or why evil things happen to good people, but we do know that God has given us all an opportunity to have everlasting life through faith in Jesus Christ. At some point, everything will corrode, die and wither away, but in the Kingdom of God, we will live for eternity. There is no sickness, death, grief, evil or sorrow. The most important prayer we can pray is that all will receive Salvation, that all will surrender to the Lordship of Jesus Christ and in doing that, God is able to do exceedingly and abundantly above all we can ever ask or think. With every life that comes to Him, may your prayer life remain pure, fervent and consistent. Remember to keep your heart clean by daily repenting and staying free from offenses and holding grudges. May the God of our Salvation bless you richly, through the fellowship of his son Jesus Christ!

Love, Your Sister, Intercessor, Prayer Warrior
Mrs. Shaquida Ano

ABOUT THE AUTHOR

Shaquida Ano was born November 6th 1981 to Linda Howard and Michael Woods. She was born and raised in Southeast, Washington DC and was educated in the DC Public School system. Shaquida is the wife of Stephen Ano and together they have 2 children, Donnell Howard and Egypt Ano. At the young age of 12, Shaquida gave her life to Christ and at the age of 27 she rededicated her life to Christ and has since been a servant in Gods Kingdom. Shaquida has a passion to teach the heart and character of Christ, provoking and admonishing believers to make right choices and walk in the fear and reverence of God. Shaquida is called and chosen by God as a fire filled preacher and teacher of the Gospel and a prophetic intercessor with a burden for the youth, women and the lost and the broken hearted. Shaquida has overcome many childhood traumas and as a result, it is her hearts cry to see every believer overcome the traps and snares of darkness and reach their God ordained destiny.

Shaquida aspires to train, equip and empower believers to reach their greatest potential. She enjoys bringing people together for fellowship by organizing activities and events specifically for youth, women and married couples. In addition, she is the founder and President of Daughters after God's Heart Ministry. Daughters after God's Heart was birthed from a desire to teach women how to develop intimacy with God, which will produce success in every area of their life.

Shaquida is a firm believer of Mathew 6:33 **"Seek you first the Kingdom of God, and his righteousness, and all things will be added unto you"**. She is the founder and overseer of "Thy Kingdom come thy will be done Intercessory prayer line". In 2018 Shaquida became an author and published her first book titled "From Rejected to Accepted." She is a woman of God who loves God with all her heart and is committed to using her God given gifts and talents to build his Kingdom.

www.ingramcontent.com/pod-product-compliance
Lightning Source LLC
Chambersburg PA
CBHW051700090426
42736CB00013B/2468